Jane,

Make 2004 a Very
Prosperous Year! ✦

Suzanne

Financial Freedom
on $1 A Day

by

Suzanne Kirkland Kincaid

National Library of Canada Cataloguing in Publication Data

Kincaid, Suzanne Kirkland, 1953-
        Financial freedom on $1 a day / by Suzanne Kirkland Kincaid
ISBN 1-894694-27-9
        1. Financial security. 2. Investments--Handbooks, manuals, etc.
3. Finance, Personal. I. Title.
HG4527.K528 2003   332.024'01   C2003-905610-4

Editing and page design:
Kim Pearson, Primary Sources, www.primary-sources.com
Cover design: Gordon Finlay
Proofreading: Arlene Prunkl

First Printing January 2004

Printed in Hong Kong

We are committed to protecting the environment and to the responsible use of natural resources. This book is printed on 100% ancient-forest-free paper (100% post-consumer recycled), processed chlorine and acid-free; it is printed with vegetable-based inks.

Universal Peace and Prosperity Foundation, Federal Way, Washington

Granville Island
Publishing

Granville Island Publishing
212-1656 Duranleau
Vancouver, BC V6H 3S4 Canada
Tel: (604) 688-0320 / Toll free: 1-877-688-0320
www.GranvilleIslandPublishing.com

Acknowledgments

It is with sincere appreciation that I acknowledge the many adventurous pioneers who helped me launch the Universal Peace & Prosperity Experiment.

The InVeStworks success has come about through a grassroots movement to make positive changes in the world, as an example of how we can all live prosperously and peacefully in harmony with God.

Extra special appreciation to:

Sue Baliwala, founder of the FUN Network (First United *Women's* Network, thefunnet@cs.com), where I serendipitously found pioneers of like mind.

Bridget McMillan, who grasped the vision immediately, graciously and generously volunteering her valuable time to create a wonderful website for InVeStworks.

My husband Fred, who patiently educated me on how to use a computer, so I could create this innovative and exciting system.

My editor, Kim Pearson of Primary Sources (www.primary-sources.com), who skilfully saw me through this new process of writing, publishing and marketing a book.

David Werba, cofounder of One World Line, who shared a similar vision to help create a better life for *one world line.*

Carol Hanson Grey, Executive Director of *Women of Vision and Action (WOVA)* and founder of *Gather The Women,* whose goal is to unite one billion women to weave a world that works.

And Neale Donald Walsch, who allowed me to participate as a Humanity's Team Leader in co-creating a better world, and whose *Conversations with God* is empowering us all.

Disclaimer

The purpose of this book is to provide accurate information on the subjects covered. The advice contained in the material may not be suitable for everyone. The reader should investigate all aspects of any financial or business decision before committing him or herself. The author believes her sources of information to be reliable, but she neither implies nor intends any guarantee of accuracy.

Neither the author nor the publisher renders legal, financial, accounting or any other type of professional advice. Readers should seek such services from a qualified professional. Although the author believes the advice contained herein is sound, she disclaims any liability, loss or risk taken by individuals who directly or indirectly act on the information contained in this book. Mention of a company name does not imply or constitute endorsement.

Dedication

This book is dedicated to anyone
who has ever made a poor decision
because of a fear of not having enough money.

InVeStworks

Proudly Presents

*The Universal
Peace & Prosperity
Experiment*

Create a *Million Dollars*
in *Passive Residual Income*
using a *Nothing Down Technique*
and *Support Global Unity*

Would *you* like to participate?

Contents

My personal goal is to *empower* people to

Simplify life

Live in honor of God

Create a fair tax system

Fulfill their personal mission in life

Equalize the monetary system of the world

Eliminate corporate and governmental

abuse and misuse of funds

Make purchases in ecological and

humanitarian balance with the planet

Preface

Who am I and why did I write this book?

My name is Suzanne Kirkland Kincaid. Just like you, I have had many roles in life. I am a wife, mother, volunteer, and have been a small business owner for over thirty years. I am an ordinary citizen who became frustrated with the inequities of our economic system. I determined to find a better way toward prosperity.

Since childhood I have yearned to contribute toward universal peace. Now that my own children are grown I have committed my time and energy toward this goal. My vision is to empower myself and others, especially those who feel disempowered now, as we work together toward global unity.

I set out to design a system that anyone could use to create wealth, so they could use that money to support people and the planet. I trust that collectively humanity will make socially responsible decisions when empowered to do so. My system provides a way for all of us to simplify our lives and live in honor of God harmoniously in peace and prosperity.

So I studied numerous current investment strategies. I knew the Internet was a powerful tool that was rapidly advancing, uniting the world and leveling the business playing field. Through my research I developed a model system I call *InVeStworks* that anyone can use to create financial freedom starting with as little as $1 a day.

Thought to Ponder

"The possibility of stepping

into a higher plane

is quite real for everyone.

It requires no force

or effort or sacrifice.

It involves little more than

changing our ideas

about what is normal."

Deepak Chopra, MD

Author

From "Seven Spiritual Laws of Success" by Deepak Chopra, MD,
co-published by Amber-Allen Publishing and New World Library, ©1994.

I began connecting with people who shared similar visions, participating in the *Gather The Women* Initiative, and attending the inaugural Congress sponsored by WOVA held in San Francisco in 2003. I am now a proud member of Women of Vision and Action, and I am committed to living up to the name.

I am further honored to be among the first to serve as a Humanity's Team Leader with Neale Donald Walsch, author of the *Conversations with God* series. Our aim is to co-create a more loving, just and peaceful world: a world that makes sense and that works for humanity.

These are challenging goals. But we can do it, *together*! The InVeStworks model system will make a significant contribution toward that effort.

Prepare to become rich. As Mark Victor Hansen says, "The most unselfish thing you can do is to become rich so you can help more people."

I invite you to participate with me in the ***Universal Peace & Prosperity Experiment.*** Empower yourself to fulfill your personal mission in life and become a part of the solution—for all of us, for humanity and for the world.

All proceeds from this book will go to the Universal Peace & Prosperity Foundation, set up to fulfill my goals of an equitable, flourishing and sustainable global environment.

Thought to Ponder

"One startling statement of utter simplicity:

There's enough.

Can this literally be true?

Yes it can. And it is.

Our world has sufficient supply for all.

There is no lack of anything in this universe.

There is more than enough of everything

everybody needs on this planet to live

joyous, peaceful, productive and fulfilling lives.

All we have to do is share.

"There's enough"

is a truth that could change the world.

Why not start by letting it change your life?"

Neale Donald Walsch
Author

Adapted with permission from "Conversations with God" newsletter by Neale Donald Walsch.

Chapter One

There is Enough!

Read the excerpt from *"Conversations With God"* by Neale Donald Walsch on the preceding page. It may be the most powerful piece of advice you ever read.

There is enough. For everyone, forever. All you have to do is respectfully use what you need and share the rest.

"Well, it *sounds* good," you might say. But in your heart you probably have doubts. That's because at the core of our thinking is a powerful fear that there is *not* enough, and we must compete, fight or even kill each other to survive.

What if this fear is based on a fallacy? What would you do differently if you knew you would always have enough money and resources? Would you share more? Would you be kinder, more compassionate? Would you reach out to help others? Would you follow your fondest dream or greatest passion? Would you write, sculpt, make music? Would you putter in your garden? Would you spend more time with your family?

What if you didn't have to be afraid all the time? Our poorest decisions are always made out of fear. Perhaps we would make better decisions if we knew there was enough for us, and for everyone.

But not everyone can have abundance, you might say. Not *everyone*.

Thought to Ponder

"The limits of the possible

can only be defined

by going beyond them

into the impossible."

Arthur C. Clarke

Author and Scientist

Yes, they can! That's exactly what the InVeStworks model system is all about.

All of us *can* have everything we ever need. There is plenty of money and plenty of resources to take care of every need, every problem, for every person.

This book will show you a powerful method to make that "impossible" dream come true!

Thought to Ponder

"The marriage between the Internet

and people-to-people sales

will accelerate the growth of network marketing

with an unprecedented opportunity

for financial freedom."

Richard Poe

Author

*From "Wave 4 Network Marketing in the 21st Century" by Richard Poe,
Prima Publishing, ©1994.*

Chapter Two

Who can use InVeStworks?

The simple answer is: *everybody*!

The InVeStworks model system is so easy that anyone can learn it — and *all* will make money. Here are some of the people who will use InVeStworks:

Parents who want to be home for the most important job there is – raising their children to be loving, responsible adults who will contribute their gifts to the world. You can run a profitable InVeStworks model system on a few hours a week, from your own home.

Senior Citizens who want a quality retirement, one that gives them not only relaxation and financial security but the time to put their hard-won wisdom and expertise to use for a better future for generations to come.

College students who want to graduate debt-free, so they can concentrate on their new professions unburdened by fear and the driving need to make money.

People in debt struggling to maintain their standard of living, perhaps facing unemployment, a possible home foreclosure or bankruptcy. The InVeStworks model system offers a way to protect assets and pay off bills.

Those challenged by *medical conditions* who are burdened

Thought to Ponder

"...the greatest good to the greatest number

is the object to be attained."

Ulysses S. Grant

18th President of the United States

by expensive and rising health care costs, or those who cannot afford medical insurance to prevent disease and maintain their precious health.

Small Business Owners who want to offer unbeatable benefits to their employees. Small businesses often have trouble acquiring and keeping good employees because they must compete with large corporations that offer their employees stock options and other valuable benefits. Instead, small businesses can offer employees the benefit of enrolling in an InVeStworks model system and both the company *and* the employees will profit.

Network Marketing companies and their members who want to discard outdated, unnecessary marketing techniques based on fear, greed and competition, and instead embrace one based on love, sharing and cooperation. With the InVeStworks model system, incessant selling to friends and family, time-consuming meetings, or intrusive advertising such as pop-ups or spam are unncessary. Network companies can allow and even encourage their members to join others, thereby providing multiple streams of income and strengthening the companies themselves.

Independent politicians who need inexpensive yet effective methods of funding their campaigns. A political campaign costs not thousands, but millions of dollars to run. The higher the office, the more money it costs. This means that only the rich can represent us in our government, or that politicians must spend a great deal of time trying to raise money. With the InVeStworks model system, politicians can offer supporters an inexpensive yet powerful way to fund their campaigns. Plus their supporters could make money for themselves if they wished.

Pioneering Words

"Suzanne has always been a determined, visionary person. Because of her, our school district received a complete two-year FREE recycling program and a substantial cash award from the Washington State Ecology Department.

If anyone could come up with a plan to help people become more successful in life, it would be Suzanne. I am grateful that she has discovered this simple, easy-to-implement method of generating multiple income streams. This will help revolutionize the economy for the 95% of us who are not rich, but soon will be!

The ball is in motion, and I'm thankful to be involved during the initiation of the upcoming revolution!

Diane Lane
InVeStworks pioneer
Administrative Coordinator,
Federal Way Community Supper
lanegang11@msn.com

Charities or Non-Profit Organizations wanting to create income for themselves and for their donors. These organizations contribute greatly to society yet never seem to have enough volunteers or money to do their good work. They must always be fundraising, consuming valuable time that would be better used to promote their causes, whether it be eliminating disease and poverty, supporting education, cleaning up the environment, or a host of other *urgently needed* activities. With the InVeStworks model system, non-profits and charities can show their donors a way to contribute to these causes and support themselves at the same time. Rather than asking for donations, what if charities offered potential donors a product or service subscription that would pay both the donor and the charity a residual income for referring others? Donors could donate a portion of their earnings back to the charity. And when they generate enough passive income to pay their bills without having to work, they will be able to donate something more valuable than money: *time*. The InVeStworks model system makes it possible for people to give both.

Schools that want to improve the educational system without holding expensive and time-consuming bond elections and raising taxes. With the current disbursement of limited funds, teachers are not appropriately compensated and classroom sizes are far too large to provide a quality learning environment. Using the InVeStworks model system for fundraising, PTAs can lend additional financial support for these critical needs and more.

Anyone wanting to contribute to the betterment of the world. People are inherently good. When empowered and enabled, humanity will collectively make the right decisions. Once freed from the crippling fear of not having enough, we will share equitably and responsibly.

Thought to Ponder

Golden Rule:

Do unto others

as you would have them do unto you.

We *can* create the world we want. A world of beauty and abundance for everyone.

Key Point !

InVeStworks is an *experiment.*

The experiment's theory is based

on sound principles,

but it is a *theory.*

The possibility of a manned flight to the moon
started out as a theory.

It proved to be correct.

Chapter Three

What is the "Universal Experiment" and why will it work?

Briefly stated, InVeStworks is a model system that uses network marketing programs combined with the power of community to create passive residual income.

InVeStworks is spelled with a mixture of capitals and non-capitals as word play meaning we are investing in networks. The non-capitalized letters spell networks. If you encounter other unfamiliar terms or jargon while reading this book, please refer to the Glossary on page 111.

InVeStworks asks you to find a few individual partners who will continually invest with you in some affiliate network companies that require a minimum amount of time, money and resources. And that's it. You need only a few investment partners (I recommend three) and about $30 a month to invest. Then design a plan using a few companies to invest in together as a team.

An affiliate network marketing company (also called MLM, for multi-level marketing, or NWM for network marketing) sells products and/or services through their members. The members, or distributors, either refer new subscribers or sell the products or services, sometimes both, to earn commissions. Some of these companies are Internet-based and some are not.

There is no need to manage a complicated organization. You don't have to sell lots of products, attend weekly meetings,

Key Point !

The Billionaires' Secret

When you reduce things down
to the lowest common denominator,
you can't help but create the largest multiplier.

Minimum Requirements = Maximum Leverage

make daily phone calls, spend hours on the Internet, stuff envelopes, stock supplies in your garage, or harass your friends and family with intrusive marketing techniques. With the InVeStworks model system, none of this is necessary.

The three keys of the InVeStworks model system are:

• Minimum Requirements

• Maximum Leverage

• Passive Income from Passive Marketing

Minimum Requirements: A powerful feature of the InVeStworks model system is *"The Billionaires' Secret."* Billionaires are willing to reduce their profit percentage from sales so that they create the largest market share. It is the difference between Wal-Mart and an expensive department store, or between McDonald's and a five-star restaurant. Fewer people can afford to buy from the more expensive places, but nearly everyone can shop at Wal-Mart and eat at McDonald's.

Do not try for promoted levels in any program to start. That will happen naturally in time. Simply apply the minimum required to tap into the income stream and strategically place any excess. This is what keeps InVeStworks simple and easy to duplicate for your investment partners and your downline. When it is simple to duplicate it will multiply faster by sheer volume. By methodically applying this system you will surpass those who aim for superstar status and soon are not able to duplicate themselves.

Maximum Leverage: By combining this minimum requirement philosophy with a few committed investment partners who will continually invest with you in multiple programs, you have just created maximum leverage. Leverage that is multiplied exponentially.

Key Point !

The InVeStworks model system

uses

passive marketing

for

creating passive income.

Some people will do more than the minimum. Wonderful! That helps everybody even more. InVeStworks uses two strategic techniques for applying extra recruits and excess sales.

Extra Recruits: If you find another investment partner and you already have your minimum (for example, three), then "give" sponsorship of that extra person to one of your three. If your three already have their three, then have them "give" it to someone in the next level, and so on. Keep trying to give that sponsorship away as far down as you can go, *working from the top down.* Since everyone only needs to notify their three, it is easy to communicate deep into your organization in a matter of a few days. Once you reach the fourth level you might not need to worry about giving the sponsorship away as your organization by then will probably be expanding every month automatically. This is the way your network grows in depth rather than width. Many affiliate networking programs do this for you automatically, with a forced matrix structure.

Extra Sales: If you sell more than the minimum required to earn the basic residual income, then "give" the excess sales to someone at the bottom of your organization *working from the bottom up.* This way it helps the most people to get paid the quickest. It not only keeps your network strong but the company too. When people get paid quickly and easily they start telling everyone they meet about their wonderful business opportunity and have the proof to verify it — bigger paychecks. *It is far more powerful to retain members than to continually replace them.*

Passive Income, Passive Marketing: Growing your network in depth using multiple programs and the least amount of time, money and energy, creates maximum exponential growth. And it is created *passively,* because soon it will grow on its own! Your commissions amass true wealth in a short time.

Key Point !

The Power of 3

You

1	1 x 3 = 3	1
2	3 x 3 = 9	2
3	9 x 3 = 27	3
4	27 x 3 = 81	4
5	81 x 3 = 243	5
6	243 x 3 = 729	6
7	729 x 3 = 2,187	7
8	2,187 x 3 = 6,561	8
9	6,561 x 3 = 19,683	9
10	19,683 x 3 = 59,049	10
11	59,049 x 3 = 177,147	11
12	177,147 x 3 = 531,441	12
13	531,441 x 3 = 1,594,323	13
14	1,594,323 x 3 = 4,782,969	14
15	4,792,969 x 3 = 14,348,907	15
16	14,348,907 x 3 = 43,046,721	16
17	43,046,721 x 3 = 129,140,163	17
18	129,140,163 x 3 = 387,420,489	18
19	387,420,489 x 3 = 1,162,261,467	19

From Three to One Billion in just 19 steps!

Adapted from the "Gather The Women" Initiative, www.gatherthewomen.org

Why does this work? Because of the power of exponential numbers and compounded growth. When you simplify the process until it requires little or no work, it multiplies like compound interest in the bank. Passive income from passive marketing. How fast can you grow when there's not much work involved?

The InVeStworks model system is being welcomed by network companies because it works on the same basic principle behind their marketing systems. Through the power of duplication and multiplication everyone is able to make money.

The chart on the previous page shows you how quickly the small number three can turn into over one billion when multiplied exponentially. Not too many of us have a concept of how large a number one billion is. As an example, if you counted by one every second of every day non-stop, it would take you a little over eleven days to reach one million. But to reach one billion it would take you nearly thirty-three *years*!

It is estimated that each person has a direct interaction with about 250 people. That is a huge multiplier! If you have three investment partners, each with a 250-person influence, all of whom have their own 250-person networks, the numbers soon become astronomical — in the trillions, more than the amount of people there are in the world.

This is why it has also been said that everyone is only "six degrees of separation" away from anyone else in the world. We are closer than we think!

Networks explode exponentially. One person can only reach so many contacts by themselves, even with sophisticated automatic management tools. If you harness the power of your networks you do not have to spend all your time selling, annoying your friends and family and running yourself ragged.

Key Point !

Any program works if you have a network,

so build your network first.

Your network *already exists*

in your 250-person circle of influence.

Word of mouth

is the most powerful form of advertising.

InVeStworks taps into your personal network, *which already exists.* You don't have to reach a billion people to make money. You only need to reach three.

With InVeStworks you will start making money only a few levels deep, because you are adding your profits from each company together. When your matrix in a company is full (that is, you are not allowed to add more members to your downline), then you and your downline simply join over again at the bottom. Or enroll in another company.

The charts in Chapter Five show you how it is possible to make a million dollars in just one year, without adding stress to your life.

Three companies. Three partners. The power of three can change your life.

Key Point !

You are only responsible

for your three investment partners,

or those you personally sponsor.

You notify your three

who notify their three,

and so on.

This is what keeps

the InVeStworks model system

so easy to manage.

Chapter Four

How does this work?
A Step-by-Step Guide

This chapter will walk you through the InVeStworks model system step by step. This is an easy program! You will have your own InVeStworks portfolio, which you will understand and be able to manage in just a few hours a week.

Really.

Step One: Recruit Three Investment Partners

You wouldn't go into business with just anyone, would you? Of course not. You don't just want warm bodies, you want people who are excited about the opportunities that InVeStworks provides, and committed to working the system. The consistency of your investment group is imperative to the success of the InVeStworks system. That means you must find people whom you can comfortably work with. The lifetime value of your investment partners is incalculable. Treat them like gold. They *are* gold.

The InVeStworks system harnesses the power of community. But because each of you has a small group of partners that you work with, one in your upline (your sponsor, if you were recruited by someone) and three in your downline (the people you recruit), you never have to worry about managing a large, unwieldy group of people.

You probably already know at least three people who would be interested in using the InVeStworks model system. You do not

Thought to Ponder

"Take the first step in faith.

You don't have to see the whole staircase.

Just take the first step."

Martin Luther King Jr.

Minister and Civil Rights Activist

need to hassle your friends, family or associates. Simple, non-invasive marketing works best. Just give out a business card with your contact information and the title of this book. You can refer them to the InVeStworks web site, www.investworks.net, or give them a copy of this book. You don't need to "hard sell" anyone! The possibility of earning a million dollars in one year from as little as $1 a day invested will get their attention. What other investment opportunity can say the same?

Get together with selected friends, family and associates, just like the Beardstown Ladies Investment Group did. They decided to learn about investing, got together with some of their friends, worked together and beat the experts time and time again! And so can you.

Start saving $1 a day to invest and get together with some of your friends. Make a commitment to help each other. You don't have to worry about trying to understand complicated stock investments. Network and affiliate marketing programs are much easier.

Perhaps you don't know three people to invest with you. Don't let that stop you. Follow the system *as if you do*. Begin today. Make the commitment to yourself that you are going to change your life, right now. Today. You will be surprised how many potential investment partners show up.

You get to design a plan that is ideal for you, and which can be easily modified when you find your partners. The sooner you join the sooner you will reap the benefits and increase the likelihood of receiving spillover.

Spillover is a type of bonus. It means that when someone above you (your upline) enrolls someone, that person is placed

Key Point !

Any company, program or network

using network marketing

can be successfully used

with the InVeStworks model system.

under you. This may be done automatically with a forced matrix, meaning no extra work for anyone. A forced matrix is often referred to as a power matrix, because it will not allow you to go any wider than the structure is designed. It powers your network to grow in depth where the real money is made!

In other programs you must manually manage the matrix for the maximum benefit of your network. I call this a *managed structure*. However the matrix is managed, it means more commissions for you! You are now building a solid network foundation that will keep the company solid and continue to pay you for rest of your life.

The charts in Chapter Five, which show possible income examples, have been diagrammed allowing for each person to find their investment partners within one month. Since you only need three people, each with $1 a day to invest, this is an achievable goal. Many people will have their three partners within a week or a day. However, even if it takes you an entire year to find your three partners, within a few years you can be financially free starting with only $1 a day — still the most profitable investment you could make.

Step Two: Review and Select Programs

There are thousands of worthwhile and affordable networking companies. Many include participation in multiple countries. Most affiliate network programs will help you manage your money, provide business and investment education, and pay you a commission for referring the services to others. Numerous programs offer discounts and other services on gas, health care, prescriptions, vision and dental health insurance, legal assistance, auto leasing, travel vacations, custom web site packages and discount

Pioneering Words

"Since Suzanne Kincaid began her grassroots journey with InVeStworks, her system has been repeatedly recognized and honored by Internet marketing experts and others. Why? I believe it is because her proposed system is a winning Million Dollar Idea. And do Internet marketing gurus recognize a good thing when they see it? Yes!"

Debbie Drake
InVeStworks pioneer
brontesmom2000@hotmail.com

virtual shopping malls. There is now a network marketing company for nearly every product and many services. Almost everything you desire can be found on affiliate network programs that also pay you a commission to shop! You can afford to be choosy, because you only need a few of them to afford a comfortable lifestyle where you won't "have to work."

Are they expensive? No. Many have low start-up and monthly fees. Consider how much money you spend on nonessential items every day, such as eating out, cigarettes, junk food, videos, movies, computer games. Anyone can find $1 a day to invest in their future.

My personal choices for the first networking companies to invest in are online educational programs. They are often more affordable to start and can pay out a higher percentage in commissions because there is no physical product involved. You also benefit by having financial and business education from the convenience of your home 24/7.

As soon as you make a profit and/or accumulate enough money from saving $1 a day, use that money to join the next program in your customized InVeStworks model system. Start buying all your products and services from a network marketing company. You already have a network so the products won't even cost you anything! Now you can afford the most expensive companies that offer the highest quality products that are ecologically sound.

How do you find these companies? You may be contacted by someone wanting you to join their network. You may already be a member of one. Ask your friends if they know of good companies. Use an Internet search engine for "affiliate network marketing." The InVeStworks web site is another source: www.investworks.net. It is updated periodically with new and worthwhile programs.

Key Point !

Invest in companies
that have experienced
business and marketing experts
in their management team,
ecologically sound products
and mission statements
reflecting positive values.

Naturally you want to look for stable companies with a high success rate for their members. Higher commissions do not necessarily mean it is a better company. Companies need to invest some of their profits in continual research, upgrades and maintenance. If they don't make a worthwhile profit they will fold or sell out. Don't begrudge the company its profits. That is what keeps you in business.

Product-based companies cannot pay out more than 50% to the downline structure and still make a decent profit. However, Internet-based companies can easily pay in the ninety percentile range because of significantly reduced expenses. Plans with unlimited matrices actually pay more than single-based ones. (Review the "Maximum Combination Success Chart" in Chapter Five.) These plans are also easier because they automatically manage themselves for you, keeping track of your original downline and placing them into your additional matrices as you continue to grow.

Newer companies are now coming out with an even more innovative compensation structure: a reverse matrix. Your downline becomes your upline with the same network of people, so those newest to the organization benefit first when the matrix is reversed. This is truly a win-win: low entry fees, worthwhile products and advanced compensation plans where everyone succeeds in the least amount of time with the least amount of effort. A prime example of the Billionaires' Secret.

You will want a variety of programs, products and services too. Select companies whose corporate staff consists of experts in their fields. Check their credentials and read their mission statements. See if they are in line with your values. Where and how are their products made and manufactured? Are they ecologically sen-

Key Point !

Learn how to stop

unnecessary and harmful

"business as usual" techniques

that are based on fear, greed and competition.

Instead, learn to work from a base

of love, sharing and cooperation.

sitive to the needs of the planet? We certainly can't stay in business without a life-sustaining planet.

Decide which criteria are most important to you: high quality products or services, minimum requirements, compensation plans, and so on. Investigate several companies to help you select those most suitable to you and your team.

The more expensive it is to participate in a company, the more carefully you need to check it before joining. The larger your network grows the more careful consideration needs to be applied.

Networks that foster cooperation are far more successful than those promoting competition. That is why it is beneficial to have a forced matrix, which automatically grows your network in depth where the most money is made. Going wide in any organization is like going into competition with your own recruits. Growing in depth leverages your entire network with the least effort and the maximum benefit.

Don't get lured into striving for advanced placements in any company no matter how lucrative they make it sound. Only a small percentage of people can work at that level. You will naturally attain this level without any effort once your organization reaches the deeper levels. Striving to meet the continual demands of a higher level will drain you of needed energy. And if you allow your network to grow in width, or if you keep more than the minimum in sales for yourself, you will significantly reduce the power of your network. Use any excess to retain your recruits or to share in the profits with your investment team. The lifetime value of a customer or recruit is far more valuable than any one-time bonus.

Key Point !

InVeStworks uses the commission systems

of affiliate networking companies

to create wealth.

Companies can change their products

or their compensation plans at any time,

with no notice.

And so can you.

If a company no longer benefits you,

you can move your entire group

the very next month.

Don't be fooled into thinking you will have to learn all about search engines, high-tech computer tools and the use of massive auto-responders. You are wasting your time and bothering people with that foolishness. Mass auto-responders are like junk mail. Rude pop-up ads are like telemarketers calling you when you are taking a shower, putting the kids to bed or sitting down to supper. And their response rate is only in single digits!

Think smarter so you don't have to work harder. Next time you receive a marketing call or piece of junk mail, why not refer them to your web site (or mine if you do not have one) or send them a business card with your information? They would probably love to have another way of earning income if they could. Telemarketers are already good salespeople just to be able to do that job, so that makes them perfect candidates for the InVeStworks model system. Always look for the possibilities in every situation.

Companies can change their products, services or compensation plans at any time without notice. If a company no longer meets your criteria you can move your entire organization to another company that does. Remember, by notifying three who notify three per day, you can reach a network of one billion in only nineteen days. You have incredible power. Stay connected to your group and you will never have to worry about money again. Corporations will have to become more user friendly, environmentally conscientious and economically balanced. Let's take our power back!

Pioneering Words

"Suzanne Kincaid has provided us with an excellent tool to create enlightened wealth. She comes from a place of such integrity that there was no way I could ignore this opportunity. From the minute I heard about InVeStworks I could see Suzanne's vision — for the world and as a simple system to enable people to help themselves and others into prosperity. It truly excites me to be able to show others how to earn passive residual income and get their power back in times that appear to make us powerless. Thank you Suzanne and InVeStworks."

Janet Hickox
InVeStworks pioneer
Co-owner Mystik Moon Promotions
www.mystikmoonpromotions.com

InVeStworks' preferences for recommended programs:

- Simple compensation plan

- Value-based mission statements

- Affordable for the average person

- Two- or three-wide matrix, forced or manageable

- Quality products or services, ecologically balanced

- Experienced corporate staff with excellent credentials

Once you have selected three to five programs, reduce each one to the minimum requirements, organize them by preference, and start with the easiest one.

Step Three: The Enrollment Process

Okay, here we are, ready to go. This is the exciting part. Watch your network of profits grow exponentially!

Enroll in the first program you or your team has selected, following instructions for the company's enrollment process. Pay the initiation or start-up fee, and purchase the minimum of product(s) or service(s) that is required to tap into the lower level of residual income.

When you receive the product or service, use it. Learn all about its features and benefits so you can recommend it to others. You may decide that you do not like it or want it. That's okay. Discover how others may benefit from what this company offers. Find someone who could use it, or donate it to charity. You are supporting your team. These companies offer something far more valuable than products or services They offer you a passive residual income!

Pioneering Words

"The InVeStworks system is a way for me to stay at home with my children and have the ability to contribute to the financial future of my family and friends. My kids, ages six and four, are already dreaming about playing on the beaches of the world. I also believe that as a TEAM we are changing families' lives, one family at a time, by offering them a chance to create true financial FREEDOM!"

Jeannine Dygert
InVeStworks pioneer
good4u@wwdb.org

You may have to work a little in the beginning but soon you will never have to work again. You will have several streams of income coming to you every single month without having to work. There is no better or faster way to wealth and financial freedom than passive residual income.

When you enroll into your first program your sponsor will give you their Distributor Identification Number (ID#) or URL link. You will use this number or link to join the program.

Once you are registered you will receive your own ID# or URL link, which you will give to your three investment partners. Be sure to give out *your* ID# or URL links — not your sponsor's. This is very important! Your investment partners must be placed under you so you will get credit for having personally sponsored them, and will receive any bonus money offered. You have started earning commissions and you do not want to miss out on any extra credit. The initial bonus referral fees help you to earn enough money to enroll in the next company. Following this method makes it a "nothing down" technique.

Your personal team will most likely go on the first level of your compensation structure, but not necessarily. Sometimes if you are directly under someone who is a good marketer or high in a beginning matrix (at the top of the original pyramid) you may receive spillover before you enroll your own team!

Now let's move on to the next levels. We'll use an example of a 3x5 matrix to show how the process progresses.

Pioneering Words

"I am extremely impressed with Suzanne Kincaid's InVeStworks system. Anyone can do it! I've been looking for a method of producing passive residual income for over twenty years and I am convinced that this is the answer. I am so grateful to be able to afford to work at home supporting my family as a single parent. Living a life of financial freedom, that's priceless."

Karin Anderson
InVeStworks pioneer
ktaglobal.com

Level 1	You recruit 3	1 x 3 =	3
Level 2	Those 3 recruit 3 each	3 x 3 =	9
Level 3	Those 9 recruit 3 each	9 x 3 =	27
Level 4	Those 27 recruit 3 each	27 x 3 =	81
Level 5	Those 81 recruit 3 each	81 x 3 =	243
You now have 364 members in this one matrix, including you.			

Move on to the second level. Have your three investment partners enroll their three partners using their ID# or links. More commissions follow.

Now the next level will bring in their three investment partners who will go into your third level. You are growing fast!

The next level will enroll their three investment partners, which will become your fourth level.

And last but certainly not least the next round of three network investment partners will go into your fifth level, or the last level in the above example. Hooray! You can now count on a substantial return on your investment.

But wait, there's more. Begin a new matrix, whether the company manages it for you or you manage it yourself. Your network is continuing to grow so you might as well take advantage of this ever-increasing partnership, and benefit your original network.

There are three ways to follow the InVeStworks system of creating financial independence: Fast, Faster and Fastest.

As an example, let's say that your InVeStworks custom system consists of five programs that require a minimum of three partners each, and you do not yet have your three partners.

Pioneering Words

"This is it! A system that is so simple anyone can do it. By combining High Tech with High Touch marketing this is truly a win-win.

"My hat is off to Suzanne Kincaid for coming up with such a powerful prosperity-creating system. The number of lives positively impacted by this program will be staggering."

Jeff Polette
InVeStworks pioneer
jeffpolette@hotmail.com

Fast: Start saving $1 a day to invest. If you can't afford $1 a day, use a Suze Orman technique from her book, *The Courage to be Rich.* Every time (that means *every time*) you make a purchase that requires change (coins) pay it with bills. Take the change home and put it in a jar. When you have $30 saved up, start your investment portfolio. Enroll in a bonus type program where there is only a one-time or annual fee. Meanwhile find your three investment partners. As soon as you find your three investment partners it will no longer cost you anything to join other programs because you will earn commissions from their place ment under you. Continue to add programs as fast as the group can comfortably go. It's okay if they too can only start with a bonus type program. You will still create wealth faster than any other method that costs you only $1 a day.

Faster: Join the first program, adding one new program every month. Meanwhile find three investment partners. If you find your three within a month it is still a no money down technique. Whether you do or not, it is still the best savings plan available. It won't take you long to find three who would love to become debt free in less than a year.

When you find your three enroll them into the first chosen program, under you as their sponsor. As soon as you receive your credit for referring them, use that money to join the next program. Everyone will follow suit using this method. Within a few months you will have multiple streams of income that will continue to increase beyond your dreams.

Fastest: Join all five companies at once. Now find three investment partners. If you are serious about wanting financial freedom it will be easy to find three. The five companies highlighted

Key Point **!**

The InVeStworks model system works anytime:

today, tomorrow, next week, next year.

Everyone has the same equal opportunity

to join at any time.

cost about $150 a month to join and less than $100 a month. You can use this same plan or design another more suitable to your needs and budget that will be affordable for most people. Anyone who truly wants a better life can find the money to adopt this system.

Step Four: Help Out Your Downline

Now that you are in all five of your selected companies, you must continue to support your downline. You must encourage them to follow the InVeStworks model system, so that everyone benefits.

You may think this will be too hard, that no one will listen to you, or that people won't follow the system. That may be true of traditional network marketing techniques. But it is easy to follow the InVeStworks model system because you are only responsible for managing your three investment partners or those you personally sponsor.

You may have more partners than the minimum required. Or you may have more partners in some companies than in others. Ideally you want all your partners to join all the same companies. However your plan unfolds you will still be successful beyond any other investment vehicle, with a lot less risk and a lot less work.

There is no need to talk anyone into joining until they are ready. There is no pressure to "get in now." InVeStworks works today, tomorrow, next week or next year. Everyone has the same opportunity to join at any time. There is no rush to get in at the top because it will continue to recycle itself over and over again. When a matrix is full you will open another or join again.

Key Point

Would you rather have $100,000 or one penny that doubles every day for a month? $100,000 is a lot of money. You might be tempted to grab it and run! But wait. Maybe you should do some math first!

One Penny

Day 1 $.01 x 2 = $.02
Day 2 $.02 x 2 = $.04
Day 3 $.04 x 2 = $.08
Day 4 $.08 x 2 = $.16
Day 5 $.16 x 2 = $.32
Day 6 $.32 x 2 = $.64
Day 7 $.64 x 2 = $1.28
Day 8 $1.28 x 2 = $2.56
Day 9 $2.64 x 2 = $5.12
Day 10 $5.12 x 2 = $10.24
Day 11 $10.24 x 2 = $20.48
Day 12 $20.48 x 2 = $40.96
Day 13 $40.96 x 2 = $81.92
Day 14 $81.92 x 2 = $163.84
Day 15 $163.84 x 2 = $327.68
Day 16 $327.68 x 2 = $655.36
Day 17 $655.36 x 2 = $1,310.72
Day 18 $1,310.72 x 2 = $2,621.44
Day 19 $2,621.44 x 2 = $5,242.88
Day 20 $5,242.88 x 2 = $10,485.76
Day 21 $10,485.76 x 2 = $20,971.52
Day 22 $20,971.52 x 2 = $41,943.04
Day 23 $41,941.04 x 2 = $83,886.08
Day 24 $83,886.08 x 2 = $167,772.20
Day 25 $167,772.20 x 2 = $335,544.30
Day 26 $335,544.30 x 2 = $671,088.60
Day 27 $671,088.60 x 2 = $1,342,177.20
Day 28 $1,342,177.20 x 2 = $2,684,354.40
Day 29 $2,684.354.40 x 2 = $5,368,708.80
Day 30 $5,368,708.80 x 2 = $10,737,417.60

Now let's ask the same question another way: Would you rather have $100,000 or over TEN MILLION dollars? Understand the power of compounded growth!

Create multiple streams of income, just like a mutual fund. Become your own mutual fund manager. As with the stock market, a company can unexpectedly fail or not perform to expectations. But because you are participating in several companies at the same time, you will not be hurt. If a company is no longer working to your benefit, replace it with another. There are thousands of companies who would love to have your business.

Stay connected to your partners. When someone drops out the network is weakened. Motivated successful people are much less likely to drop out. Staying power is a critical element in networks because they are slow to pay off. So be selective when choosing your investment partners.

Study the chart on the previous page. Notice that it takes a third of the time for the penny doubling itself to reach a mere $10. The next third of the time it escalates to over $10,000. The real power is in the last third, when it explodes to over 10 *million* dollars!

This is why you must have staying power in your group. If you do not make it easy for people to stay in, they give up too early. Not always because they want to. Most of the time they run out of time, money, enthusiasm or energy. Life gets in the way.

But if you *only* require and *always* reward the minimum they can stay in. If you support and encourage them, helping them out when they need it, they can stay in. And when they stay in, not only they win, but you do too.

You can grow very fast if you highlight the minimum requirements of the company and allow your recruits to grow at their own pace, trusting that you will do as much as you can to help them strategically with your excess.

Thought to Ponder

"There is always room at the top

for as many people

who desire to get there."

Suzanne Kirkland Kincaid

For as long as everyone stays in, you will continue to earn a maximum passive residual income with a minimum amount of work in the shortest amount of time.

And within one year you could be financially free! You might even be a millionaire.

Thought to Ponder

"Ever notice that the simplest ideas
make the most money?"

Wendy Little
Author and Philosopher

The InVeStworks System
Easy as 1, 2, 3 ...

Month 1
1. Find 3 Investment Partners (IPs) and enroll in Program 1
2. Enroll your 3 IPs into Program 1
3. Have your 3 IPs enroll their 3 IPs into Program 1

Month 2
1. When you receive $ from Program 1, join Program 2
2. Enroll your 3 IPs into Program 2 when they receive $ from Program 1
3. Have your 3 IPs enroll their 3 IPs in Program 2 as soon as they receive $ from Program 1

Month 3
1. When you receive $ from Program 2, join Program 3
2. Enroll your 3 IPs into Program 3 when they receive $ from Program 2
3. Have your 3 IPs enroll their 3 IPs in Program 3 as soon as they receive $ from Program 2

Month 4
1. When you receive $ from Program 3, join Bonus #1
2. Enroll your 3 IPs into Bonus #1 when they receive $ from Program 3
3. Have your 3 IPs enroll their 3 IPs in Bonus #1

Month 5
1. When you receive $ from Bonus #1, join Bonus #2
2. Enroll your 3 IPs into Bonus #2
3. Have your 3 IPs enroll their 3 IPs in Bonus #2

Months 6-12
Watch your network and your bank account grow! Each person only needs three investment partners. When people see you being so successful they will want to join too. This will help you and your entire organization grow even faster!

Congratulations! You are now Financially Free!

Thought to Ponder

"There is one thing stronger

than all the armies of the world,

and that is an idea whose time has come."

Victor Hugo

Author

67

Chapter Five

Where is the Proof?

The InVeStworks model system is an *experiment*. As of the time this book went to press, it had not been "proven" except in theory. Why wait an entire year to share this incredible possibility? I want everyone to share in this opportunity as soon as possible.

Everything new starts out as a theory. With InVeStworks there is so little risk and the possibility of such a high reward that it is foolish not to try it. Surely you can risk $1 a day to create the kind of life you dream about. How many investment theories offer these claims starting with $1 a day?

The following charts are examples of five companies currently offered today. These particular programs were selected because they are:

- two- or three-wide forced matrices

- low entry and subscription fees

- operated by experienced and successful Internet marketers

- online education which can pay back the highest commission

These programs offer valuable products and services and have good mission statements. But the real reason they are so

Thought to Ponder

"Most people believe
it is better to give than to receive.
The natural laws of the Universe, however,
state that there must be
an equal exchange between energies.
One cannot give without receiving,
and conversely one cannot receive without giving.
By practicing receiving with gratitude,
you train the Universe to give you more."

T. Harv Eker

Author and founder of Peak Potentials

From "Speed Wealth" by T. Harv Eker, Peak Potentials Publications, ©1996.

beneficial is they offer a high income opportunity for the average person without a lot of hard work.

These charts do not necessarily represent what any one person will earn in the indicated time frames. They are merely examples of what a person could earn if each person enrolls three investment partners within one month each, throughout the entire commission structure.

The Combination Balance Chart on pages 84-85 shows you how you might progress by joining one company per month. The Maximum Combination Chart on pages 86-87 graphs maximum potential by everyone joining all five at once, using all of your expanding network base, and rejoining programs as designed.

It's okay if your plan doesn't unfold exactly like these suggest. Just go at your own team's pace. Success is just around the corner either way. Start working your plan and you will achieve success. More than you can imagine. The ultimate purpose of InVeStworks is to help people live a better life and in turn help others. There are many networking programs available and they will work within the InVeStworks model system too.

Success Chart
Five Program Examples

Program	Entry Fee	Monthly Fee	Business Partners	Minimum Time	Monthly Income
Program 1 Unlimited 3x3 Matrices	$25	$25	3	3 months	$222
Program 2 2x15 Matrix	$25	$15	2	15 months	$77,360
Program 3 Unlimited 3x5 Matrices	$40	$40	3	5 months	$3,510
	One Time Fee				*Total Income*
Bonus 1	$35		3	10 months	$88,602
Bonus 2	$25		3	9 months	$29,538

The chart on the previous page is an overview of the five selected example programs. They show what is possible assuming all participants have three investment partners who find their three investment partners within one month each.

These are realistic results if you follow the InVeStworks model system.

Program 1: $25 can turn into $222 per month in three months.

Program 2: $25 can turn into $77,360 per month in fifteen months.

Program 3: $40 can turn into $3,510 per month in five months.

Bonus 1: $35 can turn into $88,602

Bonus 2: $25 can turn into $29,538

Combine these into one simple system to create over a million dollars a year, every year, in passive residual income.

It is possible. Don't worry whether it will work for you. Just find your three and help your three find three, and so on, until your commission structure is complete. Who cares if it takes you three years, five years, or even fifteen years to complete?

What other investment opportunity can create that kind of leverage so effortlessly and easily starting with only $1 a day?

Success Chart
Program 1

Mo.	Description	Debit	Credit	Balance
	Subscription Fee New Referral Bonus	<$25>	 $60	<$25> $35
1	Monthly Commission (3 @ $8 each)		$24	$59
2	Monthly Fee Monthly Commission (3x3=9 @ $1 each)	<$25>	 $9	$34 $43
3	Monthly Fee Monthly Commission (9x3=27 @ $7 each)	<$25>	 $189	$18 $207

Matrix is already full!

Your income from this point on is $222 per month
($189 + $9 + $24 = $222)

Unless ...

You keep that one and start another one
When that is full keep both and start another one
Keep doing this as many times as you want

Maximum Income: *infinite*

Program 1 Summary

Products:

- Hi-fidelity web-based courses on internet marketing
- Daily live online training sessions conducted by experts
- Meet and learn from other online entrepreneurs

Compensation and fees:

- Realistic monthly earnings potential
- $25 start-up fee
- $25 per month
- 3 x 3 forced matrix
- Unlimited earnings potential

Success Chart
Program 2

Level	Members	Payout	Payout on Level	Monthly Income	Referral Income
1	2	10%	$3	$3	$10
2	4	20%	$12	$15	$5
3	8	6%	$7	$22	
4	16	4%	$10	$32	
5	32	4%	$19	$51	
6	64	4%	$38	$89	
7	128	10%	$191	$280	
8	256	2%	$77	$357	
9	512	2%	$153	$510	
10	1,024	10%	$1,531	$2,041	
11	2,048	2%	$612	$2,653	
12	4,096	2%	$1,225	$3,878	
13	8,192	4%	$4,899	$8,777	
14	16,384	4%	$9,798	$18,574	
15	32,768	12%	$58,786	$77,360	

Yearly Residual with 15 Full Levels = $928,323

Program 2 Summary

Products:

- Professional web hosting
- Make money university
- Venbot auto-responders
- Online educational library

Compensation and fees:

- Pays commissions for referrals
- $25 start-up fee
- $15 per month
- Entry fees upgrade to Gold to receive commissions
- 2 x 15 forced matrix

Success Chart
Program 3

Bonus: 3 x $20 = $60			
Level	*Members*	*Payout on Level*	*Monthly Income*
1	3	$3	$9
2	9	$8	$72
3	27	$1	$27
4	81	$3	$243
5	243	$13	$3,159

Matrix is already full!

Your income from this point on is $3,510 per month
or an annual residual income of $42,120.

$9+$72+$27+$243+$3,159 = $3,510 per month
$3,510 x 12 = $42,120 per year

Unless ...

You keep that one and start another one
When that is full keep both and start another one
Keep doing this as many times as you want

Maximum Income: *infinite*

Program 3 Summary

Products:

- Personal and business web site builder

- Aeon flash builder

- Phone system

- Video conferencing

Compensation and fees:

- Realistic monthly earnings potential

- $40 start-up fee

- $40 monthly fee

- 3 x 5 forced matrix

- Unlimited earnings potential

Success Chart
Bonus #1

Month	Description	Outgo	Income
	Subscription Annual Fee	$35	
	Bonus Referral Income		
	1x3 @ $6 each		$18
1	Referral Commissions		$6
2	Referral Commissions		$18
3	Referral Commissions		$27
4	Referral Commissions		$81
5	Referral Commissions		$243
6	Referral Commissions		$729
7	Referral Commissions		$2,187
8	Referral Commissions		$6,561
9	Referral Commissions		$19,683
10	Referral Commissions		$59,049

Referral commissions: Month 1: $2 per person. Months 2 through 10: $1 per person per level.

Total Income: $88,602

Matrix complete! Now buy another one.
Start all over with your *same* network of investment partners!
Unlimited earning possibilities!

Bonus #1 Summary

Products:

- Spam-blocking software

Compensation and fees:

- Pays commissions for referrals
- $35 annual fee
- Lump sum paid out over time
- 3 x 10 forced matrix
- Unlimited earnings potential

Success Chart
Bonus #2

Level	Members	Payout on Level
	Bonus: $15.00	
1	3	$3
2	9	$9
3	27	$27
4	81	$81
5	243	$243
6	729	$729
7	2,187	$2,187
8	6,561	$6,561
9	19,683	$19,683

Collected: $29,538.00

Matrix full
Now start again!

Bonus #2 Summary

Products:

- Contact list builder
- Lead generator software
- Newsletter software

Compensation and fees:

- Pays commissions for referrals
- $25 one-time fee
- Lump sum paid out over time
- 3 x 9 forced matrix
- Unlimited earnings potential

Thought to Ponder

"There is more money being created

and available today than ever before.

The problem is, money is invisible.

Today the bulk of it is electronic.

So when people look for money with their eyes,

they fail to see anything.

Most people struggle to live

paycheck to paycheck and yet,

1.4 trillion dollars flies around the world everyday

looking for someone who wants it."

Robert Kiyosaki

Author

*From "Cash Flow Quadrant" by Robert Kiyosaki, Warner Books Publishing,
©1998.*

Let's put all five of these programs together now, month by month. The following two pages show you your expenses and income if you joined one program a month for five months and each person enrolled their three investment partners in one month each. Notice that you are never out of pocket for more than $25!

After 14 months, you could have made over *four hundred thousand dollars.* And from then on, you could be earning a residual income of a million dollars per year!

As shown in the examples, your total earnings could be:

Programs

Program 1: $222 per month

Program 2: $77,360 per month

Program 3: $3,510 per month

Total Program Income: $81,092 per month

Annual Program Income: (81,092 x 12): $973,104

Bonuses

Bonus #1: $88,602

Bonus #2: $29,538

Total Bonus Income: $118,140

Programs & Bonuses

Program Income: $973,104

Bonus Income: $118,140

Total Annual Income: $1,091,244

These are examples, showing possibilities only. There are no guarantees that you will receive this amount.

Success Chart: Combination Balance

Month	Description	Debit	Credit	Balance
1	Program 1 (P1) Enrollment Fee	-$25		<$25>
	P1 Referral Bonus *3 @ $20 each*		$60	$35
2	Program 2 (P2) Enrollment Fee	-$25		$10
	P2 Referral Bonus *3 @ $ 5 each*		$15	$25
	P1 Monthly Fee	-$25		0
	P1 Commissions		$24	$24
3	Program 3 (P3) Enrollment Fee	-$40		<$16>
	P3 Referral Bonus *3 @ $20 each*		$60	$44
	P1 Monthly Fee	-$25		$19
	P2 Monthly Fee	-$15		$4
	P1 Commissions		$9	$13
	P2 Commissions		$6	$19
4	Bonus 1 (B1) Annual Fee -$35			<$16>
	B1 Referral Bonus *3 @ $6 each*		$18	$2
	3 Programs Monthly Fee	-$80		<$78>
	P1 Commissions		$189	$111
	P2 Commissions		$18	$129
	P3 Commissions		$9	$138
5	Bonus 2 (B2) One-time Fee	-$25		$113
	B2 Referral Bonus *3 @ $5 each*		$15	$128
	3 Programs Monthly Fee	-$80		$48
	P1 Commissions (Full Matrix)		$222	$270
	P2 Commission		$30	$300
	P3 Commissions		$72	$372
	B1 Commissions		$6	$378
6	3 Programs Monthly Fee	-$80		$298
	P1 Commissions (Full Matrix)		$222	$520
	P2 Commissions		$100	$620
	P3 Commissions		$27	$647
	B1 Commissions		$18	$665
	B2 Commissions		$9	$674
7	3 Programs Monthly Fee	-$80		$594
	P1 Commissions (Full Matrix)		$222	$816
	P2 Commissions		$300	$1,116
	P3 Commissions		$243	$1,359
	B1 Commissions		$27	$1,386
	B2 Commissions		$27	$1,413

Month	Description	Debit	Credit	Balance
8	3 Programs Monthly Fee	-$80		$1,333
	P1 Commissions (Full Matrix)		$222	$1,555
	P2 Commissions		$750	$2,305
	P3 Commissions		$3,159	$5,464
	B1 Commissions		$81	$5,545
	B2 Commissions		$81	$5,626
9	3 Programs Monthly Fee	-$80		$5,546
	P1 Commissions (Full Matrix)		$222	$5,768
	P2 Commissions		$2,700	$8,468
	P3 Commissions (Full Matrix)		$3,510	$11,978
	B1 Commissions		$243	$12,221
	B2 Commissions		$243	$12,464
10	3 Programs Monthly Fee	-$80		$12,384
	P1 Commissions (Full Matrix)		$222	$12,606
	P2 Commissions		$4,000	$16,606
	P3 Commissions (Full Matrix)		$3,510	$20,116
	B1 Commissions		$729	$20,845
	B2 Commissions		$729	$21,574
11	3 Programs Monthly Fee	-$80		$21,494
	P1 Commissions (Full Matrix)		$222	$21,716
	P2 Commissions		$19,000	$40,716
	P3 Commissions (Full Matrix)		$3,510	$44,225
	B1 Commissions		$2,187	$46,413
	B2 Commissions		$2,187	$48,600
12	3 Programs Monthly Fee	-$80		$48,520
	P1 Commissions (Full Matrix)		$222	$48,742
	P2 Commissions (Full Matrix)		$77,360	$126,102
	P3 Commissions (Full Matrix)		$3,510	$129,612
	B1 Commissions		$6,561	$136,173
	B2 Commissions		$6,561	$142,734
13	3 Programs Monthly Fee	-$80		$142,654
	P1 Commissions (Full Matrix)		$222	$142,876
	P2 Commissions (Full Matrix)		$77,360	$220,236
	P3 Commissions (Full Matrix)		$3,510	$223,746
	B1 Commissions		$19,683	$243,429
	B2 Commissions (Full Matrix)		$19,683	$263,112
14	3 Programs Monthly Fee	-$80		$263,032
	P1 Commissions (Full Matrix)		$222	$263,254
	P2 Commissions (Full Matrix)		$77,360	$340,614
	P3 Commissions (Full Matrix)		$3,510	$344,124
	B1 Commissions (Full Matrix)		$59,049	$403,172

Success Chart
Maximum Combination

These figures are estimated and rounded. There are no guarantees of receiving this amount. It is merely an example of what is possible.

Program	P1	P2	P3	B1	B2	Total
Enrollment Fee	$25	$25	$40	$35	$25	$150
Monthly Fee	$25	$15	$40			$ 80

Month	Members	P1	P2	P3
Bonus		$60	$15	$60
1	3	$24	$6	$9
2	9	$9	$22	$72
3	27	$189	$40	$27
4	81	$444	$100	$243
5	243	$1,332	$340	$3,159
6	729	$3,996	$700	$7,020
7	2,187	$12,432	$2,700	$21,060
8	6,561	$37,296	$4,000	$63,180
9	19,683	$111,888	$20,000	$189,540
10	59,049	$336,108	$77,360	$568,620
11	177,147	$1,008,324	$696,240	$1,712,880
Total		$1,512,102	$801,523	$2,565,870

No Money Down Technique: If you have your three investment partners within the first month it doesn't really cost you anything. You pay $25 to join the first company, but get paid back $60 in bonus referral credits. From then on you will use your income to pay all expenses.

From Zero to Millionaire in One Year

Using a Nothing Down Technique!

The Maximum Combination Chart shows what may be possible by utilizing your same ever-expanding network with the unlimited matrices programs and continuing to start new matrices.

Wow.

B1	B2	Total
$18	$15	$168
$6	$3	$48
$18	$9	$130
$27	$27	$310
$81	$81	$949
$243	$243	$5,317
$729	$729	$13,174
$2,187	$2,187	$40,566
$6,561	$6,561	$117,598
$19,683	$19,683	$360,794
$59,049	$18	$1,041,155
$18	$3	$3,417,465
$88,602	$29,559	WOW

**WOW
Total earnings
in one year:
$4,997,674.00!**

Pioneering Words

"WOW! InVeStworks is a program that *will* change the world. Perfect for those who have very little time or money to invest."

Dr. Denice Moffat
Michael L. Robison
InVeStworks pioneers
www.namasteunlimited.com

Chapter Six

But What About ...?
22 Frequently Asked Questions

1. Is this a pyramid scheme?

No. Pyramid schemes merely exchange money and do not offer products or services. They are illegal. Affiliate network marketing programs are not pyramid schemes. Their matrices *are* pyramid shaped; it's interesting to note that pyramids are one of the strongest man made structures. They have lasted for thousands of years. See the "real" question below.

2. Is the InVeStworks model system legal?

Yes. You are buying subscriptions to legitimate affiliate programs that will pay you a rebate (commission) for referring others who also purchase a subscription. InVeStworks merely simplifies the process of network marketing. Think of InVeStworks as a custom designed "mutual fund" that you manage yourself.

3. I've been burned on "great deals" that sound too good to be true; how do I know I won't get burned with this one too?

Your maximum "risk" with the InVeStworks model system is about $30. And it is not really a "risk" at all, since you are receiving products or services for your money. If a company does not meet expectations you can cancel at

Thought to Ponder

"Many of life's failures
are people who did not realize
how close they were to success
when they gave up."

Thomas A. Edison
Scientist and Inventor

any time without further obligation. In the unlikely event that you create no income using the InVeStworks model system, you still *cannot* get burned.

4. What happens when my downline is full, or my matrix is maxed out?

Easy! Many programs allow you to start over with a new matrix. This will require an additional set-up fee and is a powerful thing to do. Your original matrix will continue generating commissions for you, as will your second matrix. When that is filled, why not a third? Some programs will enroll you in another matrix automatically, and some you must do yourself.

5. What if there is a weak link and one of the team members does not keep in contact with their downline?

Weak links are always possible, of course. With the InVeStworks model system they are unlikely. You only need to find three lifetime partners who are serious about wanting to improve their lives. They in turn need to do the same. You never ask anyone to do more than the minimum required, and you help them to do that. If this mindset is adhered to throughout your group, the drop-out rate should be very small. However, if a person does stop communicating, drop out, or die, then you would need to find a replacement for that person, and enroll them at the bottom on the matrix. If you cannot find a replacement, then you would have to accept less money.

6. What if someone just completes a third of a matrix and then stops?

Then he or she would make less money. Maybe they'd only make as little as $200 a month in passive residual income,

Thought to Ponder

"They always say that time changes things, but you actually have to change them yourself."

Andy Warhol

Artist

year after year — and they started with only around $30. Well, it's not a million dollars, but it's still not a bad return on investment, is it?

7. What if I, or a person in my matrix, become unhappy with a particular company? If I change, does everyone in my upline and downline have to change? How do I make that happen?

An important feature of the InVeStworks model system is the consistency of your network. This is what gives you leverage. So yes, if you change, you must communicate your reasons to your downline and your upline (through your sponsor). Then if you must move, move the entire network. Another option is to find a replacement for the drop-out.

8. How much time do I have to spend on InVeStworks? Will it take up too much of my personal time?

Applying the minimum requirement philosophy of the InVeStworks model system means you do not need to spend more than a few hours a week on your start-up efforts in order to be successful. And after you get going, even less than that. It is true that traditional network marketing was difficult and did take a lot of personal time, in constant recruiting, attending training meetings and seminars, and in doing paperwork. That was why most people dropped out, and few people made money. But because the InVeStworks model system recommends you *just* do the minimum required and *only* manage your three investment partners, the time drain no longer exists.

Thought to Ponder

"You can achieve anything you want in life
if you have the courage to dream it,
the intelligence to make a realistic plan,
and the will to see that plan through to the end."

Sidney A. Friedman
Speaker and Author

9. *What if I just want to join one company, not more?*

This is possible, but one of the things that makes the InVeStworks model system so powerful is that it creates multiple streams of income. Diversification is good. The affiliate companies that you subscribe to are separate companies. If one company develops problems, or is bought out, or goes under, you do not go under with them.

10. *What if my networking company says I'm not allowed to participate in another networking opportunity?*

Some network marketing companies have restrictions about marketing another networking opportunity to other members. You will need to work within their policies. You are allowed to market other networking companies to people that you personally sponsored. The reason companies do not want members to associate with another company is because they are afraid they will lose membership and sales. However, InVeStworks works in harmony with any other company as *an additional source of income* within the same network base.

11. *How can I find good affiliate network companies to invest in?*

You can ask your friends and associates if they know of any good programs. There are so many that nearly everyone will know of at least one. Or check the InVeStworks website, www.investworks.net. Or go to a search engine and type in "affiliate network marketing." You can even read your own junk mail for ideas!

Key Point !

Simply Network

to Net Worth

on $1 A Day!

12. How do I research companies and opportunities?

Review their web sites in detail. Check out the experience and credentials of their corporate staff. Study their product offerings and services. Review their compensation plans. See if their mission statement is in line with your values. Refer to the guidelines on page 51.

13. I don't need the products or services. Do I have to use them?

No. Although you will want to invest in companies with good products and services, their referral compensation plan is equally important. Think of it as a tea-drinker investing in Starbucks stock. Even though they don't drink coffee, they earn money if Starbucks' stock goes up. The products or services may not have to go to waste. You may be able to donate them to someone or a charitable organization.

14. Do I have to use the programs in this book in order to succeed?

No. The InVeStworks model system does not depend on any particular program. You can use this system with the programs you are already in, or find other ones. It will still work. After all, there are six billion people on the planet and they can't all shop at just one store!

15. Where does the income actually come from? How and when will I get paid?

The income comes from the companies you subscribe in or join. Some will pay you a referral bonus for recruiting others. Some pay a commission on your sales. And some do both. Each company has different compensation plans and

Pioneering Words

"Within minutes of reviewing Suzanne Kincaid's InVeStworks concept, I knew I had found my online passive income source. If you too are looking for cash flow to fund your ministry, independent from sporadic giving habits, I sincerely encourage you to explore this investment strategy."

Cindy Colombi, MDivCE
InVeStworks pioneer
www.TheReadyWriter.com

policies. Carefully review each so you can keep track of your earnings. Most of them do an excellent job of explaining their compensation plans. Online companies rarely pay by check. Most prefer to pay by electronic deposit using various online payment service companies. They are safe to use. Some offer debit cards too. I recommend you use a credit card when possible.

16. Will I get a 1099 form from each of the companies I join? What about appropriate taxes?

The programs that ask for your social security number or tax ID number may send 1099s. Whether they send them or not, you are responsible for tracking your earnings and paying all appropriate taxes. You need to educate yourself on current tax deductible investments. Assemble a team of accounting and investment advisors as soon as possible. Consider setting up a foundation. Investigate worthwhile charitable organizations that carry tax benefits. Make the most of your earnings.

17. Do I need a business license to earn commissions from any company?

I have not yet found a company that requires you to have a business license, however it is a good idea. There are many tax advantages to operating as a business, and licenses are easy to obtain. You may even want to start your own foundation. (See NHF in Resources.) Be sure to check with your tax advisor and State Department of Licensing, and follow all tax guidelines for the state and country in which you reside.

Thought to Ponder

"Some men see things as they are
and say why.
I dream of things that never were
and say why not?"

George Bernard Shaw
Author

18. Will I be contributing to spam?

The InVeStworks model system emphatically does not recommend spam. Some companies offer opt-in lists of leads and the use of auto-responders. They are a waste of time. There is no need to use auto-responders unless you have a valuable product and only send it to viable prospects who could truly benefit from that service or product. Otherwise please don't use them. Just get together with a few of your friends. Word of mouth is a much more effective method of attracting clients.

19. Is there a guarantee that I will earn a million dollars in a year?

No. How fast anyone grows depends on them. The examples given in the charts give you an idea of how you might progress and when you *could* reach the million dollar a year mark.

20. Has anyone made a million dollars using the InVeStworks model system?

Not yet. At publication, the original InVeStworks group has not been together for an entire year. The income we have made so far is right on track to our goals. What the InVeStworks model system offers you is an opportunity to participate in an experiment, and create your own network for financial freedom.

21. Why do you spell InVeStworks with a mixture of caps and non-caps?

InVeStworks combines "invest" and "networks," because we are investing in networks. The non-capitalized letters spell "networks."

Thought to Ponder

"I can't do the things that you can do.

And you can't do the things that I can do.

But together we can do great things."

Mother Teresa

22. Where can I go to ask further questions or get help using the InVeStworks model system?

Use the resources listed in this book, as well as the Helpful Hints and these FAQs. Refer to the InVeStworks web site www.investworks.net, where you can download more information and expanded charts for your personal use. Send us a note at the Contact Us link to let us know how you are progressing. We'd love to hear about your successes and include them as testimonials in the follow-up book next year.

Key Point !

The chart below is an excellent example of the power of circulating money from a simple purchase. Joycebelle compiled a book of poetry, *A Tribute to Our Beloved, 9/11,* honoring the memory of those who died. She donated the book to charities at a recommended retail price of $7.97. Realize the value:

Simple Facts about Charitable Giving, Buying Power, and Paying for our Government

If every person in the United States bought just one book for $7.97, this would boost the economy by over two billion dollars:

276,000,000 Americans x $7.97 = $2,199,720,000

If every person in the United States bought just one book with a profit margin of $2.97 per book and a tax base of 20%, income taxes paid to the U.S. government would be over 163 million dollars:

$2.97 x 276,000,000 = $819,720,000 x 20% = $163,944,000

If every person in the United States bought just one book with a profit margin of $2.97 per book and a 5% state tax rate, state taxes would be over four million dollars:

$2.97 x 276,000,000 = $819,720,000 x 5% = $4,098,600

If each book purchased was shipped via U.S. mail at the cost of $1 per book, the added revenue to the U.S. Postal system would be over 276 million dollars:

276,000,000 x $1.00 = $276,000,000

If you consider that the population of the United States only represents 6% of the world population, the possibilities are endless!

Giving Definitely Goes Beyond Money.

Copied with permission from www.joycebelle.com. "A Tribute to Our Beloved, 9/11" is also available in two special editions: "Freedom Forever for Kids"; and "Freedom Forever - a Special Military Edition." Books are available as hardbound, softbound or e-books, and are ideal for fundraisers.

Chapter Seven

What Now?

Now that you have created wealth, what will change in your life? Change is often uncomfortable at first, even good change. Now you are free. You have the freedom to come and go as you please, do what you want to do, with whom you want, when you want, where you want, how and if you want. Now there are no excuses for not achieving your dreams.

From the very first day you begin the InVeStworks model system, plan on being rich. Think about the wonderful contributions you could make to the world with an extra million dollars a year, every year of your life.

Really think about it.

Yes, you will be able to purchase nice things, for yourself and your loved ones. But this is the least important part of wealth.

You will also be able to spend significant time with your children, your spouse, your parents, your siblings, your friends — those you love. You will be able to strengthen the bonds of family and community.

You will be able to pursue your talents and interests. Now your dreams and passions can become reality. Now you can contribute your unique gifts to the world.

Thought to Ponder

"It does not take a lot

to make a lot,

build a lot,

prosper a lot

in thought and deed

and give a lot

to all those in need."

Joyce Belle Edlebrock

Author and Publisher

From www.joycebelle.com, Rich World Inc., www.richworldpublishing.com

And most importantly, you can *give back*. You can make the world a better place — for all of us.

If you have followed the InVeStworks model system for a year, you probably will have more money than you need. So give it away! Imagine what good your favorite charity could do with an extra $200 a month, or $2,000 a month, or even $200,000 a month!

I have shown you a way to radically increase your income while freeing up your time. Now will you commit to giving ten percent of your time and money to make the world a better place?

This is the entire purpose of the InVeStworks model system.

We all know that the world needs critical care right now. Many organizations such as The Union of Concerned Scientists have been warning us for decades that we are destroying sustainable life. I don't say this to scare you but to wake you up. We all need to pull together and fix the massive problems we have created.

This is easier than you think. My favorite analogy is to compare the world with a family of five whose house is a big mess. Someone important calls and says they will be over in fifteen minutes. Yikes! What will they do? They'll never get that mess cleaned up in time.

Oh yes they will. They will divide up the chores and go to work. One person takes the kitchen, another the dining room, another the living room, another the bedrooms and another the bathrooms, and that house will be in a presentable condition in fifteen minutes.

Let's do that with the world!

Thought to Ponder

"Responsibility is the key to human survival.

It is the best ground on which to build

world peace, an equitable sharing

of the world's resources,

and the development of true respect

for the environment

on behalf of future generations."

The Dalai Lama

Are you concerned that our wetlands are disappearing and wildlife is threatened? Are you upset that the oceans are polluted? Great! Now you have the money — go do something about it! Contribute to environmental organizations. Help to preserve a wetland in your own community. Volunteer your time and money to clean up the national forests, or the coastlines, or the oceans. Or a thousand other things.

Do you want to help the poor, indigent or homeless? Great! You've got the money — now go help them! Pay a family's electricity bill for one year. Give money to a homeless shelter. Buy and donate clothing. Open and staff a job-training center. Or a thousand other things.

Do you want to help eliminate cancer or AIDS or arthritis or any other disease? Great! You've got the money — now make the elimination of that disease your priority! Donate money to hospitals or scientific research centers. Purchase advertising spots to raise public awareness. Find a struggling medical student and pay for their education. Or a thousand other things.

Remember the power of exponential numbers! What if we *all* took just ten percent of our income and time and used it to better the world we share? How long would it take before the world truly was the beautiful place it should be?

Not long. And *you* can make it happen.

Pioneering Words

"At last. This is a program that can work for anyone! Perfect for the NON-salesperson. We are so grateful our friends shared InVeStworks with us.

We're telling everyone about how easy it is to duplicate the steps to "Enlightened Wealth" and claim their Pot of Gold!"

Jackie and Robert Smith
InVeStworks pioneers
jackiesmith9935@sbcglobal.net

Glossary

Affiliate network marketing: The business model for a company that markets products or services through affiliates (members) who are paid commissions on three or more levels, for recruiting new members and/or product or service sales. Also known as multi-level marketing, network marketing, MLM and NWM.

Affiliate marketing: Affiliate companies pay on only one or two levels. They are not considered network marketing or multi-level marketing programs because they do not pay on three or more levels.

Auto-responder: A software program that automatically delivers information by e-mail. Many networking companies offer auto-responder programs to help their members market via the internet. Do not participate in spam or invasive marketing if you use auto-responders. The InVeStworks model system does not require auto-responders to be successful.

Compression: The process of moving all positions upward periodically to fill in any holes where members may have dropped out in the upline matrix. This is usually beneficial. You will need to refer to the company's policies to find out if they use this procedure and how often. With the InVeStworks system, this will rarely be necessary as most people will stay in because of the simplicity, unity and rapid profitability.

Thought to Ponder

"I would rather have
1% of the efforts of 100 people
than 100% of my own.

"If you can count your money,
you're not a billionaire!"

J. Paul Getty
Billionaire

Downline: All the people who join a particular affliliate networking program after you in your specific compensation structure. This includes your three investment partners, who you are responsible for communicating with. Your downline is important because you not only earn commission from people *you* refer to a program, but also people your referred customers refer, and people those customers refer, and so on and so on, up to the number of levels in a particular matrix.

Exponential numbers: Also known as geometric growth or progression. This is what bankers are referring to when they speak of "the miracle of compound interest." Remember the penny a day example: if you start with one penny, and double it every day for 30 days, at the end of the month you will have *over ten million dollars*!

Forced matrix: Each of the levels in your downline has a specified number of positions. A forced matrix ensures that when the positions on each level are filled, any new customers get automatically rolled down to the next level, meaning that no work is required to manage your network. For example, when you sign up your three people, your entire first tier is filled. If you sign up one more person, that person will go to one of the positions on your downline's second level, under someone on your first level.

Invest: Using your money to participate in an enterprise offering the possibility of profit. With the InVeStworks model system, you are investing in networks, or subscribing to affiliate network programs. You subscribe to affiliate marketing programs at the minimum level, establish a downline of three investment partners, and receive compensation for referring others. The profit from your investment is the compensation you receive for referring others.

Thought to Ponder

"Out of abundance,

he took abundance

and still abundance remained."

The Upanishads

Leverage: When people use their skill and effort to help other people in their organization succeed, they are creating leverage. When you add more than one network, you multiply that leverage. The more people you help, the more people you will have in the organization, and the bigger your residual income will be. Your influence and effectiveness is much greater as part of a network than as an individual. No matter how hard you work or how talented you are, what you can achieve by yourself is limited by the hours in a day. But if you leverage your time through a network, there is virtually no limit to how many people your message can reach.

Managed structure: An InVeStworks method of placing excess sales or recruits for maximum benefit for the most members and the company. You manage the compensation plan by placing extra recruits to grow in depth rather than width, and extra sales beyond the minimum requirement to the lowest level available. This strengthens your network by allowing the maximum numbers of members to earn the most commissions. This strengthens the company because now more members can afford to stay in. *It is far more profitable to retain members than to continually replace them.*

Matrix: Commission structures for affiliate network marketing programs are usually in the form of a matrix. This is the pyramid shaped grouping of the people who invest in programs as your team, and your team's teams. You will be paid commissions on all the sales or referrals from people in the downline of your matrix. Matrices are described by how many positions and levels are allowed in a particular program.

Minimum subscription level: The least amount of money or involvement required to become a member of a program and receive residual commissions.

Thought to Ponder

"If one advances confidently
in the direction of his dreams
and endeavors to live the life
which he has imagined,
he will meet with a success
unexpected in common hours."

Henry David Thoreau
Author and Philosopher

MLM (Multi-level-marketing): Another name for network marketing or affiliate marketing. See affiliate network marketing.

Networking: A gathering of acquaintances or contacts; the building up or maintenance of relationships, especially with people who could bring advantages such as business opportunities.

Network marketing or NWM: Another name for affiliate marketing, network marketing or multi-level marketing. See affiliate network marketing.

Passive residual income: Residual income is continuing income that you receive after the work you have done to produce it has ended. An example of residual income is royalties paid to authors and musicians. Passive residual income is paid to you without your investment of any more time or effort. A simple example of passive residual income is the interest you earn from your savings account. Passive residual income is the most powerful form of income.

Pyramid scheme: A pyramid scheme is illegal, and refers to companies that merely exchange money and do not offer products or services for sale. The InVeStworks model system is NOT a pyramid scheme.

Reverse matrix: A reverse order of the normal matrix. New members are brought in from the top down in reverse order.

Spillover: When people in an upline refer new members after their first level is full, the new members "spill over" to the next level. See forced matrix.

Sponsor: The person who recruited you and who is responsible for communicating information to you from their upline.

Pioneering Words

"From the minute I met Suzanne, I was struck by her vision. She developed InVeStworks as a near fail-proof system for creating financial freedom. Finally, there's a dynamite combination of excellent affiliate programs and a simple money-producing system. This offers real hope for anyone who is struggling to keep his or her head above water."

Bridget McMillan
InVeStworks pioneer
bridget.mcmillan@verizon.net

Upline: The people in your upline are those who joined a particular program before you. They include your immediate sponsor.

Thought to Ponder

"May we spend tomorrow
in the magical state of imagination!
Together let us dream a future of
balance, partnership, justice and peace
where everyone's gift is welcome
and where all life is honored."

Carol Hansen Grey

Executive Director, "Women of Vision and Action"

Founder, Gather The Women

Women of Vision and Action (WOVA) www.wova.org
Gather The Women Initiative (GTW) www.gatherthewomen.org

Resources and Helpful Hints

Recap of Key Points:

• Any program works if you have a network, so build your network first.

• InVeStworks promotes finding your three investments partners in your existing network, your own circle of friends and acquaintances.

• Word of Mouth is the most powerful form of advertising.

• InVeStworks works even if you don't have a network already in place, because it is easy to find three partners willing to invest with you.

• With InVeStworks, each person only needs around $30 and three investment partners to start. Simple. Easy. Affordable.

• Any network company can use the InVeStworks model system, which I call the *Seven Steps to Enlightened Wealth*. *1. Unite* with three investment partners. *2. Review* all suggested programs. *3. Reduce* each one to its minimum requirements. *4. Organize* in order of preference. *5. Start* with the easiest one. *6. Add* additional programs. *7. Use* the money for something good.

• Be respectful of other networks. Don't try to talk someone into leaving a company to join yours. Simply offer yours as another stream of income.

Key Point !

Focus on the minimum requirement.

Don't strive to be a superstar.

• Focus on the minimum requirement. Don't strive to be a superstar.

• The easier it is the larger the market share. *When you reduce things down to the lowest common denominator you can't help but create the largest multiplier.*

• Networking companies are based on the power of compounded growth.

• Even if you don't have any investment partners, join at least one program or a few bonus programs. Start on the road to financial freedom. This is the best savings plan you can invest in. Now find three investment partners and begin adding programs as soon as you can with the profits.

• You will never need more than three people, but if you find another investment partner, great! Strategically give extra recruits to your downline *working from the top down.* Help those that have been in the longest to get their three as quickly as possible. If your programs use forced matrices, this will be done automatically.

• You will never need to sell more than the minimum, but if you do that's great! Strategically give the extra sales to someone on the lowest level, *working from the bottom up.* This helps the most people to get paid faster so they can afford to stay in until they are self-funded by the programs. You can't stay in business very long if you aren't making any money.

• Give excess sales and extra recruits to your downline to help them succeed faster.

Thought to Ponder

"*Ecolonomics* is a new and powerful idea.

We can do justice to our planet

and we can enhance corporate profitability

if our decisions are based squarely

on enlightened values."

Dennis Weaver

Actor, Activist and Author

From "All the World's A Stage" by Dennis Weaver, Hampton Roads Publishing, ©2001

•   The InVeStworks model system uses passive marketing for creating passive income.

•   Work from a base of love, sharing and cooperation.

•   The income produced by the programs is of equal importance to the products or services.

•   Companies can change their products or their compensation plan at any time. If they no longer benefit you, you can move your entire group and become profitable right away in a new program.

•   You must have multiple streams of income. If one or two programs fail, you have other income streams to make sure you remain wealthy.

•   Invest in companies that have experienced business and marketing experts in their management team, and that have mission statements reflecting positive values.

•   You are only responsible for your three investment partners, or those you personally sponsored. You notify your three who notify their three, and so on. This is what keeps the InVeStworks model system so easy to manage.

•   The InVeStworks model system works anytime: today, tomorrow, next week, next year. Everyone has the same equal opportunity to join at any time.

•   People are inherently good and will make the right decisions when empowered and enabled to do so.

•   It's called an Experiment. You are merely asked if you would like to participate in the experiment. What is the risk to *not* try it?

Pioneering Words

"I was moved when I heard about Suzanne's purpose for her book and the InVeStworks model system. Her goals were right in line with my own. Seeing that her system works for anybody and everybody was exciting. I am proud and honored to be a part of this team. I am anxious to do my part in assisting to create world peace by helping people be financially free so they can focus on their life purpose. This is truly a beautiful system!"

Thayne Westerman
InVeStworks pioneer
worldvisionteam@msn.com

Blank Forms:

These Program Information forms will help you keep track of pertinent information for each program. Use them as a guide to give out to your recruits. Specific details will vary with each company. Be prepared with two or three alternate user names in case your choice is already used. Remember to keep your password secrct. Fill out one form for each company you join.

Program Information Form
Name
Email
Username
Password
Address
Phone
Credit Card #
Expiration
CVV# *(3-4 #s on back of credit card)*
Name on credit card
Billing address on card
Online Paying Service Acct #
Notes

Pioneering Words

"Suzanne Kincaid has hit the mark! For years I knew in my heart that something was greatly needed to promote significant change on the planet. This is it! Now we can truly empower ourselves to be who we really want to be.

With InVeStworks, we WILL create a better world."

Dakara Kies
InVeStworks pioneer
Dakara Kies Co. Holistic Products for Health
www.dakara.com

Sponsor's Affiliate Links

Sponsor's Name _____

Sponsor's Phone Number _____

Sponsor's Email _____

Program 1 Sponsor
URL Link _____

Program 2 Sponsor
URL Link _____

Program 3 Sponsor
URL Link _____

Bonus 1 Sponsor
URL Link _____

Bonus 2 Sponsor
URL Link _____

Pioneering Words

"Suzanne, thank you so much for all the hard work you put into InVeStworks, the most incredible investment system out there. I read all the time about how we should work smarter, not harder, but until InVeStworks I had not found a system in which this was truly possible.

"For those of us who are not great networkers, InVeStworks is a true blessing! I am so excited about the future, not only for myself but for all those who I will be able to help."

Saylor Niederworder
InVeStworks pioneer
saylor@seetobelieve.net

Pioneers' companies:

InVeStworks pioneers are participating in some of the following networking companies.

$1.67 a day	Nature Sunshine Products
Atomania	New Vision
Cash Culture	New World Team
Cell Tech	Neways International
Chocolate Riches	Nikken
DHS Clubbucks	Oasis (Medialine)
Ecoquest	Pampered Chef
Everyday Wealth	Pro List
Ezinfocenter	Prosperity from the Inside Out
Freestore Club	Rainforest Herbs
Get Moving Today	Spam Terminator
Global Travel International	Stampin' Up
ICallSMART	The Greatest Networker
Isagenix	The Limu Company
Life Force International	The Master's Miracle
Mannatech	Total Marketing Live
Market America	Travel Works International
Melaleuca	Trilogy Group
Moneyhome	World Lending Group
Multi-Pure Corporation	Young Living Essential Oils

The mention of these companies does not constitute recommendation or endorsement.

Thought to Ponder

"There is nothing more tragic
than to see people who have
sold themselves short
on what is possible in their lives.

"Take time to discover possibilities,
and the dreams will be priceless."

Robert Kiyosaki
Author

From "Guide to Investing" by Robert Kiyosaki, Warner Books Publishing,
©2000

Books to Read:

The Soul of Money
by Lynne Twist

The New Revelations
by Neale Donald Walsch

Rich Dad, Poor Dad series
by Robert Kiyosaki

The 9 Steps to Financial Freedom
by Suze Orman

The Miracle of Tithing
by Mark Victor Hansen

The Seven Spiritual Laws of Success
by Deepak Chopra

It's Hip to Help the Homeless
by Richard Tripp

Games to Play:

The Cashflow Game
http://media.richdad.com/cashflow4_teaser.html

The Prosperity Game
http://www.projectprosperity.org/projectprosperity

Thought to Ponder

"We need to teach

the next generation of children from day one

that they are responsible for their lives.

Mankind's greatest gift,

also its greatest curse,

is that we have free choice.

We can make our choices

built from love or from fear."

Elisabeth Kubler-Ross

Author

Causes to Consider:

The Institute of Ecolonomics devotes its resources to creating a symbiotic relationship between a strong economy and a healthy ecology as the only formula for a sustainable future.
www.ecolonomics.org

The Hunger Site is a leader in online activism and a dynamic force in the fight to end world hunger.
www.thehungersite.com

Humanity's Team bases its activities on the messages in the *Conversations with God* series of books by Neale Donald Walsch.
www.humanitysteam.com

Gather the Women's mission is to demonstrate a new way of world leadership, based on partnership, cooperation, harmony and balance.
www.gatherthewomen.org

The National Heritage Foundation will manage your foundation for maximum benefit.
www.nhf.org

The Union of Concerned Scientists augments rigorous scientific analysis with innovative thinking and committed citizen advocacy to build a cleaner, healthier environment and a safer world.
www.ucsusa.org

Thought to Ponder

"Our lives begin to end
the day we become silent
about things that matter."

Dr. Martin Luther King, Jr.
Minister and Civil Rights Leader

InVeStworks
Seven Steps to Enlightened Wealth

1. *Unite* with three investment partners.

2. *Review* suggested programs.

3. *Reduce* each to the minimum requirements.

4. *Organize* in order of preference.

5. *Start* with the easiest one.

6. *Add* other programs as soon as possible.

7. *Use* that money for something good!

Here's YOUR Pot of Gold!
There's one for EVERYBODY!

Thought to Ponder

"Never doubt that a small group of thoughtful,
committed citizens can change the world.
Indeed, it's the only thing that ever has."

Margaret Mead

Anthropologist and Author

InVeStworks Pioneers

Terri Allen
Wendy Amendola
Karin Anderson
Wesley Antholz
Pearl Atchison
Lorraine Ballantine
Donald Barnett
William Bass
Paul Berentsen
Karen Louise Bobrowski
Lori Bockwoldt
Jeannette Bray
Linda Brookings
Kellie Brooks
Joanna Bruno
Marty Bryson
Cindy Burcher
Valerie Campbell
Greg Chamberlain
Vivek Chandrahasan
Ron Clarkson
Cindy Colombi
Sarah Conlin
Carole Conlon
Lisa Cook
Diego Cornejo
Dr. Patricia Crane
Al Davis
Lola Davis
Jutta DeLeon
Ron DeMers
Brian DiNielli
Julie Dittmar
Ellen Dennis
Debbie Drake
Jim & Jeannie Dygert

Mary Ellen
Sue Ellen
Eugene Eng
Nicole Engel
Carol Ann Feucht
Catherine Foster
Joel Friant
John Fuller
Randy George
Neil Getty
Sarah Gilmore
Richard Glanville
Angel Grace
Anne Marie Grant
Donna & Gordon Gremmert
Cindy Gremmert-Moseid
William Hanson
Karin Harrison
Janet Hickox
Dennis Hodge
Nicholas Hodge
Zora Jackson
Scott Johnson
Dakara Kies
Fred Kincaid II
Oneida Kirkland
Richard Konotopetz
Krista & Rich Landers
Rick & Sheree Landers
Chris Lane
Diane Lane
Tracy Lane
Kathryn Lange
Henry Latta
Robert LeBow
Ann Lee

Thought to Ponder

"Imagine all the people living life in peace.

You may say that I'm a dreamer,

but I'm not the only one.

I hope someday you'll join us,

and the world will live as one."

John Lennon

Singer-Songwriter

InVeStworks Pioneers

Craig Lewis
Emy Lewis
Wendy Lewis
Delaine Macku
Michael & Angie Madsen
Skip Madsen
Maggie Mann
Michael Marier
Travis Mathews
Bridget McMillan
Claude Michaud
Halina Miller
Dr. Denice Moffat
Saylor Niederworder
Wendy Neill
Kathi Ogawa
Vanessa Pace Ministries
Michael Parker
Dianna & Frank Parrick
Jeff Polette
Bill Rauscher
Cherri Rettler
Michelle Richmond
Don Roberts
Michael Robison
Fred Rodgers
Claude Rogers
Michele Rogers
Ruth Rosebrook
Leann & Jeff Rowe
Jennyfer Russ
De Etta Ryan
Vanessa Sandford
Ivy Santos
Christine Scheppele
Dan & Mary Scheppele

Shane Scheppelle
Mary Sebastiani
Vicki Simcox
Garry Smith
Jackie & Robert Smith
Joshua Smith
Laura Sterling
Vanessa Stewart
Mark Stiles
Susan & Ty Stone
Molly Straub
John Swidrovich
Richard Swift
Faith Szafranski
Virginia Taylor
Bruce Ternes
David Tesney
Jerry Tilley
Wayne Tkatchuk
Garrett & Roshael Tomsin
Sarah Tuttle
Diane Underwood
Star & Jason Valenti
Shannon Walter
Mary Jo Warren
Terri Weller
Melanie Wells
Gwen Welty
David Wernecke
Thayne Westerman
Richeal Wheeler
Robert Whisnand
Ruth Whitney
Dave Woodsworth
Janiece Wright
Charles Zito

Thought to Ponder

"When the solution is simple,

God is answering."

Albert Einstein

Scientist

143

Personal Notes